Understanding the Process of Economic Change

Douglass C. North
Professor of Economic History,
Washington University, St. Louis, Missouri

Twenty-eighth Wincott Memorial Lecture delivered at Bishop Partridge Hall, Church House, Westminster, on Monday, 12 October 1998

The Trustees of the IEA have agreed that any surplus over costs arising from the sale of this Paper should be donated to the Wincott Foundation.

Published by the Institute of Economic Affairs for The Wincott Foundation, 1999

First published in March 1999 by
The Institute of Economic Affairs
2 Lord North Street
Westminster
London SW1P 3LB

© The Wincott Foundation 1999

Occasional Paper 106
All rights reserved
ISSN 0073-909X
ISBN 0-255 36422-9

Printed in Great Britain by
Hartington Fine Arts Limited, Lancing, West Sussex
Set in Times Roman 11 on 13 point

Contents

Foreword
by SIR GEOFFREY OWEN

THE LINK BETWEEN NATIONAL INSTITUTIONS AND ECONOMIC PERFORMANCE has preoccupied economists and economic historians for many years, and the issue has acquired even greater importance following the end of the Cold War. As former totalitarian countries have made their halting progress towards democracy and the market economy, prescriptions offered by outside advisers have often taken insufficient account of the absence of institutions and traditions which are taken for granted in the West. An apparently attractive reform such as privatisation needs, if it is to be successful, to be embedded in a set of institutional arrangements which allows prices and markets to work freely within a generally accepted legal framework. Another recent event which has brought these institutional questions to the fore has been the Asian economic crisis. Why has the much-admired Asian economic model run into such difficulties? One possible explanation is that the institutions and policies which were appropriate at one stage in a country's development – when it was catching up with the West – lose their usefulness when the economy approaches maturity. The challenge then becomes one of institutional adaptation, and it has proved extremely difficult for countries to break out of systems and practices which served them well in the past.

Few economists are better qualified to advance our understanding of these matters than Professor Douglass North. He has devoted most of his academic life to the study of institutions and institutional change, and he has shown in a number of stimulating books and articles how history influences the choices open to countries as they seek to develop their economies, and why some choices have worked out better than others. North's research combines detailed historical investigation with insights drawn from modern economic theory, and the results have been path-breaking. The trustees of the Wincott Foundation were delighted that

Professor North accepted their invitation to deliver the 1998 Wincott lecture, and this paper contains the text of his talk.

As was shown in the discussion which followed the lecture, Professor North raised many questions to which no final answers are yet available. He showed, for example, how the success of Western economies has depended in part on a set of institutions which made co-operation in impersonal exchange worthwhile. But this 'immense achievement', as he puts it, has evolved over six or seven centuries – these countries have learned how to adapt their institutions to shocks and crises. How other countries, with their very different starting points and different histories, can achieve the same adaptability, and do so in a much shorter time span, lies at the heart of many of the current controversies about economic development.

As in all IEA publications, the views expressed are those of the author, not of the Institute (which has no corporate view), its Trustees, Advisers or Directors. We are grateful to Professor North for his contribution to this debate, and for improving our knowledge of the process of economic change.

February 1999   SIR GEOFFREY OWEN
                                                    Chairman of Trustees
                                                    The Wincott Foundation

The Author

DOUGLASS C. NORTH, CO-RECIPIENT OF THE 1993 NOBEL MEMORIAL PRIZE in Economic Science, has spent more than 50 years pondering complex variations of a simple question: Why do some countries become rich, while others remain poor? Born in Cambridge, Massachusetts, Professor North graduated with a triple BA degree in political science, philosophy, and economics from the University of California at Berkeley in 1942, and later, in 1952, received a PhD degree in economics there. He served as a US Merchant Marine from 1941 to 1946, and was an instructor in celo-navigation from 1944 to 1946.

He began his academic career at the University of Washington in Seattle where he spent 33 years as a member of the economics faculty, including a 12-year tenure as department chair and five years as director of the Institute for Economic Research. He was the Peterkin Professor of Political Economics at Rice University in 1979, Pitt Professor of American Institutions at Cambridge University in 1981, a Visiting Fellow of the Center for Advanced Studies in the Behavioral Sciences at Stanford University, and currently a Hoover Institution Senior Fellow.

He joined the faculty of Washington University in 1983 as the Henry R. Luce Professor of Law and Liberty in the Department of Economics, and served as director of the Center in Political Economy from 1984 to 1990. He was president of the Economic History Association for one year, editor of the *Journal of Economic History* for five years, and served for 20 years as a member of the Board of Directors of the National Bureau of Economic Research. In 1987, he was elected to the American Academy of Arts and Sciences, and, in 1992, he became the first economic historian ever to win one of the economics profession's most prestigious honours, the John R. Commons Award, which was established by the International Honors Society in Economics in 1965. He was elected a Fellow of the British Academy in July 1996, and installed as the first Spencer T. Olin Professor in Arts and Sciences at Washington University in October 1996.

Professor North has lectured at most major American and European, and many Asian, universities. He is the author of more than 50 articles and eight books. His current research includes property rights, transaction costs, economic organisation in history, a theory of the state; the free rider problem; has focused on the formation of political and economic institutions and the consequences of these institutions on the performance of economies through time. That research was published by Cambridge University Press in *Institutions, Institutional and Economic Performance* (1991).

Understanding the Process of Economic Change

DOUGLASS C. NORTH

IT IS A GREAT PLEASURE AND AN HONOUR to share in what has become a distinguished lecture series, and I am delighted to be here, and particularly to greet some old friends whom I have known for many years.

1. A World of Dynamic Economic Change

The subject of my lecture today is Understanding the Process of Economic Change. Including 'Understanding' in the title requires a little explanation. What follows is not a theory of economic change. We are a long way from such a theory; and indeed in the neat sense of being comparable with the kinds of general theories we have in economics, such a theory is probably impossible. But understanding the process of economic change is an essential prerequisite to improving economic performance. We live in a world of dynamic economic change, but the theory we employ to understand our world is static and the tools we employ to understand and control this world are simply inadequate to deal with the issues. Nothing illustrates this better than the fumbling efforts made over the last ten years to restructure what was the Soviet, and is now the Russian, economy. Understanding involves that we rethink the process of change, and not simply tinker with static models. So this lecture is about such a rethinking. It is still a long way from complete, but it is suggestive of where I am going in the next book I am writing.

Economic change is a result of changes, *one*, in the quantity and quality of human beings; *two*, in the stock of human knowledge, particularly as it applies to the human command over nature; and *three*, in the institutional matrix that defines the incentive structure of society. A complete theory of economic change would therefore integrate these three strands. In this short talk I shall focus on the deliberate efforts of humans to control their environment, and therefore the priority is on institutional change. But there is no implication that the other two strands are not equally important, as I hope to illustrate.

The central focus of human activity has been, and continues to be, the effort by human beings to gain greater control over their lives by developing a structure to order their relationship to the environment. In effect, the ubiquitous objective has been to reduce the uncertainty that characterises that environment. Throughout most of history, the central uncertainty has been the physical environment; but as humans have increasingly gained greater control over the physical environment, with the development of science and technology, the uncertainties resulting from human interaction, the human environment, have taken overwhelming priority. Indeed it is our success in conquering the physical environment that has created a human environment of immense complexity, and thereby increased human uncertainty. Let me elaborate on this. What I have called elsewhere the second economic revolution really was the application of science to technology in such a way that it gave humans an enormously increased command over nature. That is not surprising to any of us living in this century. What we do not understand properly yet, however, is that in the process of applying science to technology, we have changed the human environment fundamentally. We live in a world in which interdependence characterises our very life. The complexities of dealing with the very different environment are central to our getting a handle on the issues with which I am concerned. The structure we impose on our lives to reduce uncertainty accumulates from prescriptions and proscriptions, which produce a complex mix of formal and informal constraints embedded in language, physical artefacts and beliefs. It is beliefs that connect 'reality' to the institutions.

2. Reality and Beliefs

The reality of a political-economic system is never known to anyone, but humans do construct elaborate beliefs about the nature of that reality – beliefs that are both a positive model of the way the system works and a normative model of how it should work. The belief system may be broadly held within the society, reflecting a consensus of beliefs; or widely disparate beliefs may be held,

10

reflecting fundamental divisions in perceptions about the society. The dominant beliefs, that is, those of political and economic entrepreneurs in a position to make policies, result over time in the accretion of an elaborate structure of institutions, both formal rules and informal norms, that together determine economic and political performance. The resultant institutional matrix imposes severe constraints on the choice of entrepreneurs when they set out to create new or to modify existing institutions in order to improve their economic or political positions. The path dependence that results typically makes change incremental, although the occasional radical and abrupt institutional change suggests that something akin to punctuated equilibrium change in evolutionary biology can occur in economic change as well. Change is continually occurring, although the rate of change will depend on the degree of competition among organisations and their entrepreneurs. Entrepreneurs enact policies to improve their competitive positions, resulting in alterations of the institutional matrix. What follows are revisions to perceptions of reality, and therefore new efforts by entrepreneurs to improve their position in a never-ending process of change. Let me illustrate this process with a very brief story of the rise and fall of the Soviet Union.

Lenin's Inspiration

Marx and Engels provided the belief system that was Lenin's inspiration, explaining the way the world was and the way the world could be. The circumstances of the war-torn Russia of 1917 provided an unusual opportunity for abrupt institutional change. While Marx provided no blueprint for the transformation or construction of a socialist society, he did provide fundamental ideological building blocks, particularly with respect to property, which remained guiding principles and constraints on Soviet leaders. After dire necessity forced retreat from those principles and led to the creation of the NEP (the New Economic Policy) in 1921, the first five-year plan in 1928 returned to ideological orthodoxy. In the early years of the Soviet Union, there was substantial discussion of alternative strategies, and hence institutions, to build socialism. The gradual accretion of the complex institutional matrix that resulted led to perceived successes (for example, in heavy industry), and failures (for example, in agriculture), and attempts to correct the failures within Marxian orthodoxy.

As the economy grew, it underwent the devastating torment of the Nazi invasion, and then the lengthy reconstruction process. The institutional matrix was continually being modified by external stimuli such as war, or internal perceptions of needed institutional alterations, guided by a belief system that evolved within the ideological limits of Marxism. The result throughout the 1950s, 1960s, and early 1970s was rapid growth of physical output, particularly in heavy industry, and military technology, and certain areas of scientific knowledge; and the advent of superpower status. Almost half the world became Socialist or Communist in this era, and Socialism or Communism was widely perceived to be the wave of the future. But then growth began to slow. The slowdown was a result of enormous increases in the costs of transacting; increasing problems of agriculture, which became ever more acute; and efforts at institutional reform to rectify the problems which became, and continued to be, ineffective in solving the problem. After the accession of Gorbachev in 1985, the policies of the next six years led to absolute decline, and in 1991 to the demise of the Soviet Union – perhaps the most striking case of rapid demise without outside intervention in all of human history.

This is a story of perceived reality, inducing a set of beliefs which in turn induced a set of institutions to shape the society, which in turn introduced at the margin incremental policies, which in turn altered reality, which in turn went back to revising beliefs. The key to the story is the way beliefs are altered by the feedback humans get from changes in perceived reality as a consequence of the policies in action, the adaptive efficiency of the institutional matrix – that is, how responsive it is to alteration – and the limitation of changes in the formal rules as correctives to perceived policy. Now it is one thing to be able to provide a summary description of the process of economic change; it is something else to provide sufficient content to this description, to give us an understanding of this process. What do we mean by reality? How are beliefs formed? How do they change? What is the relationship between beliefs and institutions? How do institutions change? How do institutions affect performance? What accounts for the widely varied patterns of performance of economies and policies, both at a moment of time and through time? And perhaps most fundamental of all, what is the essential nature of the process itself? I have nothing to add to the age-old question of philosophers, what is reality? But I do have a direct pragmatic interest in just what it is that we are trying to model in our theories, beliefs and ideology. The pragmatic concern is with the degree to which our beliefs coincide with that reality. To the extent that they do coincide there is some prospect that the policies that we enact will produce the intended result, although throughout human history, we have been wrong much more often than we have been right. It is important that we be very self-conscious about the nature of that reality. And even more important is the awareness of just how reality is changing.

3. Beliefs and Their Evolution

Beliefs and the way they evolve are at the heart of this lecture. For the most part economists, with a few very important exceptions like Hayek, have ignored the role of ideas in making choices. The rationality assumption that has served economists and all the social scientists well for a limited range of issues in macro-economic theory is a devastating shortcoming in dealing with most of the major issues confronting social scientists and policy-makers, and it is a major stumbling block to the path of future economic progress. The way we perceive the world and construct explanations about the world requires that we delve into how the mind and brain work, the subject of cognitive science. The field of cognitive science is still in its infancy, but already enough progress has been made to suggest important implications for social science theorising. The questions we must be able to answer are how human beings respond to uncertainty – and particularly the uncertainty arising from the changing human landscape. One of the dilemmas that we economists have long agreed on, and that eminent theorists like Kenneth Arrow and Robert Lucas have emphasised, is that you cannot theorise in the face of real uncertainty. You cannot theorise in the face of uncertainty because, in a world in which you do not know what is going to happen, you do not have any way to be able to derive statistically a probability distribution of outcome. But in practice, human beings theorise about the world of uncertainty all the time. We make decisions in the face of pure uncertainty, based on religious or other beliefs or ideologies. Now, what we need to know, though it is not a subject of this lecture, is how human beings actually go about making choices in the face of pure uncertainty. The subject is central to the way in which human beings throughout history have been forced to make choices when they really do not have an understanding of where they are going.

A lack of understanding has never stopped human beings from evolving complex beliefs or ideology; Marxism is one of the most elaborate belief systems that has ever evolved, and one that dominated the beliefs and the choice-making of half the world for a good part of the 20th century. But Marxists are not alone; we all have belief systems, and to the degree that we are policy-makers and we are in the midst of enacting policies, we are making policy every day with beliefs, ideologies, whatever we want to call them, which are, to put it mildly, incomplete, imperfect and uncertain with respect to their outcomes. Most of what we are doing these days in cognitive science is evolving away from a view that the mind works like a computer, which was indeed the early view of how the mind worked. Today, more and more we have come to the conclusion that the way in which the mind works is based on pattern-based reasoning. The neural networks of the mind gradually establish patterns by which they interpret the world, and the patterns become quite complex and elegant, as indeed many belief systems and ideologies are.

The patterns are important because to the degree that we face novel situations, to the degree that we face new problems that we have not faced before, then the question is: How do we make sense out of them?

4. The Institutional Structure

If the novel situation is similar enough to patterns that we have in our mind, that we have derived from past experience, then indeed we may solve the problems more or less accurately and enact policies and rules that improve our lives. To the degree that the situations are really novel, they pose fundamental dilemmas with respect to how we deal with them. Now, humans attempt to use their perceptions about the world to structure the human environment in order to reduce uncertainties in human interaction. The resultant institutional structure is a combination of formal

14

rules, informal constraints and their enforcement characteristics. By formal rules I mean constitutions, laws; by informal constraints I mean norms of behaviour, conventions, codes of conduct. Obviously the degree to which both the formal rules and informal constraints are enforced determines how effective those rules and constraints are in shaping our actions. The institutional constraints accumulate through time, and the culture of a society is a cumulative structure of rules, norms and beliefs that we inherit from the past, that shape our present, and that influence our future. Institutions change, usually incrementally, as political and economic entrepreneurs perceive new opportunities, or react to new threats, affecting their well-being. Institutional change can result from change, in the formal rules, the informal norms or the enforcement of either of these.

But whose perceptions matter? Obviously not everyone's; we need to delve into the structural rule-making in the society to answer that question. Much of the work in political economy concerns modelling the way in which we make and aggregate choices that shape incremental change in institutions, a subject that is again far away from what I can deal with here. The political/economic structure of the society and the way it evolves are the keys to whose choices matter, and how they are aggregated to shape policy.

Now let us see if we can begin to put the pieces together, to explore very incrementally, very incompletely, the process of change. We can conceive of the process as a circular flow, in which we have initial perceptions of what reality constitutes. Those perceptions in turn lead to the construction of a set of beliefs, ideologies to explain that reality and to explain the way that we should behave. That in turn leads to the creation of an institutional structure, or an institutional matrix, which then shapes our 'world'. And as our beliefs about that reality incrementally change, we enact policies that incrementally modify that institutional structure. An incremental change is always constrained by path dependence. That is, the existing institutions constrain our choices. As we make those choices which are incrementally altering policy, we are changing reality. And in changing reality, we are changing in turn the belief system we have. That circular flow has gone on ever since human beings began to try to shape their destiny.

5. A Continuously Changing World

I want to stop here to point out how my view deviates from the view of most economists with respect to this problem. The difference between the story I am telling you and the one that I see most economists telling, is that most economists believe that you can derive models based on the past, and indeed, on what we call Bayesian updating of the model; and with those therefore you can make the right policy in the present and the future. Now that works if the future is like the past. If the future is the same as the past, one could indeed make a stronger statement and say what would happen over time. Even though we made mistakes and enacted the wrong policies, the feedback would get us to correct those policies, modify them; and eventually we would arrive at a world in which our belief system and reality would coincide. But that is if the world stays the same. And that is indeed the implicit model that economists typically have. The world, however, is not staying the same; we keep on changing reality by the policies we enact, and we have been doing so for the ten thousand years about which I have been writing. This is important, because if indeed the future is different, and different in novel ways from the past, then whether we get it right or get it wrong is going to become a crucial issue. But the important thing is to recognise that if the world is changing, and if we are creating novel situations that cannot easily be dealt with, and we cannot use the same tools that we have used in the past, or cannot use them uncritically, then we are going to get it wrong in the present and the future.

Some questions we should answer, but for which we still have very incomplete answers, are the following: Is the process similar to models derived from evolutionary biology? What difference does the intentionality of the players make? And what is the nature of the human intentionality that is the immediate source of institutional change? Does the uncertainty of the human race come from the inherent instability of the human landscape or the perceptions and beliefs that we have about the human landscape? Economists at the Santa Fe Institute, which I have visited a number of times, spend a lot of time modelling what we call complexity.

Complexity, a lot of it, deals with attempting to develop chaotic models of the world. Do they characterise the world that we are trying to confront? Or indeed, is the world more orderly? Are there beliefs that make it so that we get it wrong? Or is it the reality that we misunderstand? What is the source or sources of discontinuous, abrupt evolutionary change? What is the underlying source of path dependence, how does this path dependence affect performance? Path dependence is something again that we do not know very much about. We know that it is very real; anybody who is an historian knows that we very seldom change direction abruptly. The institutions and beliefs of the past have an enormous effect on constraining the ability to make change in the present and the future. But exactly how those constraints work, when they loosen up so we are able to make more radical change and when they do not are matters that we should know a lot more about. And finally, what makes for adaptive efficiency?

6. Adaptive Efficiency

By adaptive efficiency I mean the ability of some societies to adjust flexibly in the face of shock and evolve institutions that effectively deal with altered reality. I spend time now advising transition and Third World economies. I observe that when people become excited about a country that has grown for 10 years, they say, 'It's on the path to growth', or 'We've finally overcome Latin American instability', or 'Transition economies are finally on the way'. For an economic historian, that is just ridiculous. I think in terms of 50 or a hundred years, and then I can think about whether you have really evolved a society that has the ability to withstand shock, to overcome continual problems. That is a very different thing from growing for 10 to 20 years. Western Europe and the United States are adept at what I would call adaptive efficiency. They are economies and societies that have withstood all kinds of shocks, wars and radical fundamental change, and that have managed throughout to adapt their institutional structure to make it so they have had continuous growth over long periods of time. That is what we really want to have in societies that today are Third World or are like the Latin American economies that I advise in which there has been stop-and-go growth for the last 300 years, but not steady growth. Steady growth is a very different thing, something that we do not know how to create in the short run. We do know, that here in England and in the rest of Europe, and in the United States, we have evolved an institutional structure in which the informal norms of behaviour, more important than the formal rules, have built into the body politic this adaptability. This structure tends to provide a set of guiding principles that constrain the way in which we evolve and have made for this adaptive efficiency. But we do not know how to create it in the short run. I know of no way that a country that has not had it can get it except by following the example of Western Europe. There, a long evolutionary process, over four or five hundred years, has evolved a set of institutions, both formal and informal, that has made possible a structure that has these characteristics.

7. The Depressing Tale of Economic History

How successful are we at controlling our destiny? In the tradition of Herbert Simon, who directed our attention to these issues, we can ask what difference does it make that the agents fall far short of substantively rational behaviour which would entail full knowledge of all possibilities and contingencies, the exhaustive exploration of the decision tree, and a correct mapping between actions, events and outcomes. The short answer is that it makes a lot of difference. Economic history is an endless depressing tale of miscalculation, leading to famine, starvation, deceit and warfare, death, economic stagnation and decline, and indeed the disappearance of whole civilizations. Even the most casual inspections in today's news suggest that this is not purely an historical phenomenon. Yes, we do get it right sometimes, as witness the spectacular growth of the Western world for the past four or five centuries. But we are wrong more often than we are right.

8. Why We Are So Often Wrong

Let me go over three ways we get it wrong – ways we have been wrong in the past, are wrong in the present, and will get it wrong in the future. The *first* is the straightforward one which should be clear by now: we never really understand reality. The theories, beliefs, models that we have are very imperfect; they are vast oversimplifications of a complex world, and they are usually static oversimplifications. It is not bad that they are oversimplifications, as long as we grasp, and have built into our theories, the essential characteristics that are the guiding principles that are making it work. And making it work over time is something that is much more difficult to do than to have an accurate snapshot of a moment in time. So, the degree to which we understand this reality is obviously the first place where we never get it completely right, and sometimes we have it completely wrong.

The *second* concerns belief systems. Obviously to the degree that our beliefs are attempting to make sense of a world in which we have pure uncertainty, they are unlikely to be very good or very accurate. Whether the beliefs are derived from religions, as they have been throughout most of human history; whether they are derived from elegant models, and Marxism is certainly one of the most elegant, complex, and impressive systems of theory that has ever been constructed; or whether they are *ad hoc* bits and pieces of beliefs that characterise the way in which most of us, including most politicians, make everyday choices, they mean that we are going to be wrong much of the time, particularly, as I intend to illustrate, as the world is changing on us.

The *third* way we get it wrong is one that is particularly sensitive to the world we are in today, and to the problems that economists are facing who attempt to deal with improving the lot of transition and Third World economies. And that is, that we use tools to control our world that are very blunt instruments. The only tools that we have that allow us to try to shape the world we are in, are the formal rules of the game. But the structure that guides the way in which we operate is made up of formal rules, informal norms of behaviour, and their enforcement characteristics. All we can change quickly are the formal rules. We cannot change the informal constraints, at least not in the short run; and even our ability to control enforcement is very limited. In 1990 I was one of four Americans invited by the Soviet Academy of Scientists to go to Moscow to advise the Soviet Union on its economy. The first American said, all you have to do is privatise and all will be well. The second American said, all you have to do is eliminate government, and all will be well. The third American said, all you have to do is have the computer and all will be well. I was the fourth American and I said, do not pay attention to the first three speakers; the problems are much more complicated. Let me illustrate by discussing the first panacea – privatisation.

9. Privatisation as an Example

Privatisation in these days, and indeed for some time, has been a buzzword. But anybody who watches the Soviet Union – or now Russia – has observed that privatisation without the fundamental structure of the rule of law and enforcement mechanisms to go with it does not produce anything worth a hoot. There is privatisation in Latin America, but privatisation in the context of government-fostered monopolies produces a world that does not look at all like what you want. It is a very real problem that when you are trying to improve the performance of an economy you need to change the informal constraints, and you must get enforcement characteristics that will produce the desired results.

In the early 19th century, Latin American countries gained independence, and when they did, most of them copied the US Constitution and many of the formal property rights rules that were enacted as a part of that constitution. The results were widely variant with the way in which those rules worked in the United States. This is not surprising; the rules in the United States had evolved out of the set of rules that had been part of the assemblies of the various colonies, and they were rules provided by Britain both for self-government and for assembly, and also for a set of fundamentally effective property rights. They were taken over and embodied in the US Constitution, and they were consistent with norms of behaviour and enforcement characteristics that we had evolved over previous years. The result was not surprising: they worked quite well. But when adopted by Latin American countries, they were wildly at variance with situations there. Latin America had been run from Madrid or from Lisbon, and it had viceroys that enforced the rules, the objective of which had been to gather treasure for Madrid or Lisbon; there was no self-government; and property rights, enforced only from Madrid, gave monopolies to merchants.

It is not surprising that when independence came and a set of policies was imposed that came out of the heritage of American experience that had gradually evolved it produced radically different results.

I am using Latin America for illustration, but I could equally talk about Russia, or indeed, other economies in Eastern Europe. What we are trying to deal with is how we can adjust and make changes in policies so that they produce more effective performance characteristics on the part of societies and economies. It is quite clear that our ability to make radical change depends on the way in which beliefs have evolved in society, and the degree to which sets of beliefs are amenable to the kinds of changes that we think are essential. Let me give you two illustrations: one, a general one, and then one specifically dealing with perhaps the most interesting economy in the world today, which is China.

10. The Shift from Personal to Impersonal Exchange

The general one is quite straightforward. The most dramatic and traumatic shift that has occurred to human beings throughout history has been the shift from personal to impersonal exchange. By personal exchange, I refer to a world in which we deal with each other over and over again in small-scale economic, political and social activity, where everybody knows everybody, and where under those conditions, to use a simple illustration from game theory, it pays to co-operate. That is, game theory says that human beings co-operate with each other when they play a game over and over again, when there is no end game, when they know the other parties to the exchange, and when there are small numbers. In such a world transaction costs are low, but production costs are high, because it is a world of small-scale production, without economies of scale, and in which you typically cannot use the modern technologies I have described as part of the second economic revolution.

This revolution began in Germany in the chemical industry in the second half of the 19th century and is now spreading all over the developed world. The world it has produced is characterised by impersonal exchange. It is a world in which our dependence rests upon people all over the world, whom we do not know; there are no repeat dealings; and large numbers of players are involved. Therefore it is a world in which the game is played differently. In game theory, we say such a world is one in which it pays to defect. That is, if you do not know the other party, you are never going to see him or her again, and neither side has any particular further hold on the other, it pays to run off with the money. A lot of economic historians have spent much time considering the way in which the Western world, in the last six or seven centuries, evolved a set of institutions that made co-operation in impersonal exchange worthwhile. That is, these institutions changed the pay-off so that impersonal exchange paid off and therefore people did not defect and cheat, lie and steal.

That was an immense achievement. However, the movement from personal to impersonal exchange means you have to create not only economic institutions that will do it, but political institutions as well. And indeed that is the dilemma. We know how to create economic institutions that will make for impersonal exchange, and indeed we have created a lot of them; but we do not know how to create political institutions that will do so. You have to have political institutions because when the size of the market moves beyond the realm where reputation can be an effective vehicle in constraining human behaviour, then you must have third-party enforcement and that means government and the state. And I can assure you that we do not know how to create such political systems – even though there is a lot of exciting work going on in political economy. Russia will never have sustained success until it has a polity that will produce those results. Nor will anywhere else, for that matter. And we are a long way from it. So, the movement from personal to impersonal exchange is a fundamental stumbling block.

11. The Evolution of Institutions in China

China is intriguing because it does not appear directly to do any of the right things. It certainly does not have the rule of law, it has a political dictatorship and it does not have secure property rights – all of which have undergirded the development of the United States and the Western world. But note what China has done. The central government has given, not necessarily deliberately but nevertheless given, autonomy to the local governments. The autonomy has been fed with capital coming in from overseas Chinese. The local TVEs (town-village-enterprises) are neither firms nor co-operatives, they are a weird mixture of both, but they are a mixture of both which has substantial autonomy, and for which local communist party bosses provide secure property rights. The result has been an economy which has, not in a formal but in an informal sense, evolved a set of institutions, rules of the game, that has created the highest rate of growth of any economy (though I think that China faces gigantic problems down the road). So there are lots of different ways to achieve wealth. There are lots of different ways to structure the game, to provide the correct incentives (that is what institutions are, incentive structures) to do the right thing. But, nevertheless, doing them requires a mixture that we very seldom get right.

12. Some General Implications

Let me conclude with some very broad general implications, implications that are rather at variance with what most of orthodox economics has to say. The *first* is quite straightforward, and I trust should not surprise you even if you may not agree with it: there is no way to make intelligent predictions of long-range change. And that is because we cannot know today what we will learn and believe tomorrow. I do not believe that anybody other than soothsayers can tell what is going to happen to societies and economies down the road. We may know tomorrow, the next day, a few years ahead; but what we are going to learn and believe in the more distant future is something we cannot know today.

Second, there is no such thing as *laissez-faire*. I am a big fan of Milton Friedman's, but *laissez-faire* got us off on the wrong foot completely. Any market that is going to work well is structured; it is structured by deliberate efforts to make the players compete by price and quality rather than compete by killing each other or other means. Now I want to emphasise this because throughout history and indeed in the present world there has been much talk about *laissez-faire* or getting government out of it. You do not get government out of it. What you try to get government to do – either directly by rules and regulations and property rights, or indirectly – is to structure the game so you force the players to compete by price and quality rather than compete in other ways. It means you must structure factor and product markets differently; it means you must structure a labour market, a capital market. I feel very conscious of this because for the last half-dozen years I have been an adviser to the World Bank on a set of policies in which we have attempted to look at how to structure various kinds of markets to work well. We looked at telecommunications; most recently, we have looked at water. And it has been an education. With telecommunications, just to take a simple illustration, the structure at one moment of time which might work well, is not going to be the same as at another moment of time, because technology has changed the industry from being a natural monopoly to being a competitive industry. And therefore radically different policies may be involved, with respect to the way in which you want the game structured to get the results that you want.

Now this has a lot of implications, I suggest, for the world that we are living in today, because the kind of structuring of financial and capital markets that worked well in the past simply does not necessarily work well today. For example, I am looking at what happened to Japan: over the last 40 years financial and capital markets worked well and the Ministry of Finance and the bureaucracy in Japan evolved to produce a capital market and financial structure that do not work well today. The fact of the matter is that you cannot assume that markets are going to continue to work perfectly. So we not only need to structure each market differently, but perhaps most important – and indeed the thing that makes us economic historians essential – is, we must recognise that if we structure the way we did yesterday, it does not necessarily mean it is going to be well structured today or tomorrow. Technologies change, competitive structures change, government policies change, and the way in which they operate change. If we are going to have markets that work well tomorrow, we must be continually concerned that they are going to adapt to new problems and new strategies.

The foregoing is all too brief a summary of the process of economic change. I do hope it will inspire scholarly efforts to carry forward a research agenda that I believe to be essential to improving the performance of economies through time.

The Wincott Memorial Lectures

1. **The Counter-Revolution in Monetary Theory**
   MILTON FRIEDMAN
   1970 *Occasional Paper 33*   5th Impression 1983   £1.00

2. **Wages and Prices in a Mixed Economy**
   JAMES E. MEADE
   1971 *Occasional Paper 35*   Out of print

3. **Government and High Technology**
   JOHN JEWKES
   1972 *Occasional Paper 37*   Out of print

4. **Economic Freedom and Representative Government**
   F.A.HAYEK
   1973 *Occasional Paper 39*   3rd Impression 1980   Out of print

5. **Aspects of Post-war Economic Policy**
   LORD ROBBINS
   1974 *Occasional Paper 42*   £1.00

6. **A General Hypothesis of Employment, Inflation and Politics**
   PETER JAY
   1976 *Occasional Paper 46*   2nd Impression 1977   £1.00

7. **The Credibility of Liberal Economics**
   ALAN PEACOCK
   1977 *Occasional Paper 50*   Out of print

8. **Economists and the British Economy**
   ALAN WALTERS
   1978 *Occasional Paper 54*   £1.00

9. **Choice in European Monetary Union**
   ROLAND VAUBEL
   1979 *Occasional Paper 55*   £1.00

10. **Whatever Happened to Productivity?**
    GRAHAM HUTTON
    1980 *Occasional Paper 56*   Out of print

The Dilemma of Democracy:

The Political Economics of Over-Government

Arthur Seldon

1. Economists' notions of 'public goods' have provided the intellectual backing for the expansion of government-provided goods and services.
2. Governments have taken control of activities – 'public' goods, 'public utilities', welfare, local government services – which would have been better left to the private sector: they were mostly being privately provided before being crowded out by the state.
3. If government does not withdraw from many of its functions, people will increasingly escape to non-state suppliers. They may also refuse to pay for state activities they regard as superfluous.
4. Government will have to reduce its share of national income from over 40 to nearer 20 per cent.
5. 'Democracy' today generally represents the tyranny of the majority. Organised groups extract favours from government at the expense of those who are unorganised, unschooled or unskilled. Even worse, the people are incited to thwart their long–term interests by snatching short–term gains.
6. Attempts to correct market 'imperfections' create over-government. The '...evidence of history is that the imperfections of government are more deep-rooted and less remediable than the imperfections of the market.' Government 'remedies' begin too soon, go too far and carry on too long.
7. As government has grown too large, people have found means of escape - for example, by the 'parallel economy', by barter to avoid taxes, by electronic money, by the Internet and by taking advantage of liberalised trade and modern communications to use facilities in other countries without moving home.
8. A new mercantilism is emerging as government, to preserve its position, tries to regulate industry and commerce, including labour. But the market, which gives the power of exit, will outlast politicised alternatives.
9. Government must accept that it has lost the power to maintain its economic empire. 'The escapable power of political government..' is up against '...the irresistible economic force of the market.'
10. The remaining decision for government is to '...arrange its retreat with dignity before the escapes multiply to deprive it of the authority to influence the rate of its withdrawal.' Hobbes' warning has been trumped by Spinoza's vision.

The Institute of Economic Affairs

2 Lord North Street, Westminster, London SW1P 3LB
Telephone: 0171 799 3745 Facsimile: 0171 799 2137
Email: iea@iea.org.uk Internet: http://www.iea.org.uk   ISBN: 0 255 36417-2

£10.00

Corporate Governance:

Accountability in the Marketplace

Elaine Sternberg

1. Businesses and corporations are not the same thing: not all corporations are businesses, and most businesses are not corporations. Whereas 'business' designates a particular objective, 'corporation' designates a particular organisational structure.

2. Corporate governance refers to ways of ensuring that corporate actions, assets and agents are directed at achieving the corporate objectives established by the corporation's shareholders (as set out in the Memorandum of Association or comparable constitutional document).

3. Many criticisms of corporate governance are based on false assumptions about what constitutes ethical conduct by corporations, and confusions about what corporate governance is.

4. Protests against takeovers, 'short-termism', redundancies and high executive remuneration are typically objections to specific corporate outcomes, not criticisms of corporate governance.

5. Many misguided criticisms of the Anglo-Saxon model come from confusing corporate governance with government: it is a mistake to criticise corporations for not achieving public policy objectives, and for not giving their stakeholders the rights and privileges commonly associated with citizenship.

6. Some criticisms of the traditional Anglo-Saxon model of corporate governance are justified. There are serious practical obstacles that prevent shareholders from keeping their corporations and corporate agents properly accountable.

7. Though commonly praised, the German and Japanese systems are considerably less capable of achieving the definitive purpose of corporate governance than the Anglo-Saxon model is. Neither is designed to protect, nor typically used for protecting, property rights.

8. The increasingly popular stakeholder theory is also incapable of providing better corporate governance. Stakeholder theory is incompatible with all substantial objectives and undermines both private property and accountability.

9. Regulation that attempts to improve corporate governance by limiting shareholders' options, and reducing their freedom to control their own companies as they choose, is necessarily counterproductive.

10. The way to respond to flaws in current Anglo-Saxon corporate governance mechanisms is to improve the accountability of corporations to their ultimate owners, preferably by having corporations compete for investment, and institutional investors for funds, in part on the degree of accountability they offer to their beneficial owners.

The Institute of Economic Affairs

2 Lord North Street, Westminster, London SW1P 3LB
Telephone: 0171 799 3745 Facsimile: 0171 799 2137
E-mail: iea@iea.org.uk Internet: http://www.iea.org.uk

ISBN 0-255 36416-4

£12.00

Regulating European Labour Markets:

More costs than benefits?

John T. Addison and W. Stanley Siebert

1. The present British government has signed on to the social chapter, the provisions of which are now an integral part of the European Union treaties .

2. European Union social policy can be traced back at least to 1974 even though the treaty basis for social legislation is very narrow.

3. The extension of majority voting under the 1986 Single European Act made it easier to pass social legislation. After the 'social charter' was proclaimed in 1989, legislative proposals 'came thick and fast', some making 'creative use' of health and safety criteria.

4. The 1997 Treaty of Amsterdam not only contains the provisions of the earlier Agreement on Social Policy but includes an employment chapter which '...opens up scope for considerable Commission activism in the future' and is a '...central plank of social policy'.

5. Market failure arguments may provide a basis for political intervention in the labour market but they are not clearcut. Furthermore, it is difficult to specify mandates which will deal adequately with market failures and government corrective action will itself be subject to failure.

6. Britain and other countries with less regulated labour markets have been better at creating employment opportunities than the more regulated major EU states.

7. Empirical studies generally show that the net effect of employment protection and similar rules is '...lower employment, greater and longer unemployment for some and, implicitly, a decline in the speed with which labour relocates from declining to growing sectors of the economy.'

8. Not all employment regulations will have the same effect. But the 'upward harmonisation sought by the Commission' has potentially serious costs in terms of 'disemployment and reduced employment growth'.

9. The Commission has failed to meet its obligation to evaluate the possible effects of its social proposals on the labour market. Its efforts have been amateurish and have taken place in an 'analytical vacuum'.

10. Its proposals should in future be subject to independent efficiency audit, not to prevent the development of social policy but to provide information on the employment and other consequences of new mandates.

The Institute of Economic Affairs

2 Lord North Street, Westminster, London SW1P 3LB
Telephone: 0171 799 3745 Facsimile: 0171 799 2137
E-mail: hwu@iea.org.uk Internet: http://www.iea.org.uk   ISBN 0-255 36420-2

£8.00

The Changing Fortunes of Economic Liberalism:
Yesterday, Today and Tomorrow

David Henderson

1. Liberalism implies '...restricting the powers and functions of governments, so as to give full scope for individuals, families and enterprises.' But the state has an important role in '...establishing and maintaining a framework in which markets can function effectively...'

2. The doctrine of economic liberalism goes back about two and a half centuries. Over that period there has been no consistent trend towards liberal economic policies: indeed, liberalism was generally in decline over the hundred years up to the late 1970s.

3. But in the last two decades many governments have adopted reform programmes which have liberalised their economies and international transactions have been freed. The Economic Freedom of the World project, for example, shows a clear trend towards liberalisation in many countries - especially since 1985.

4. Few, if any, countries which have embarked on economic reform in the last twenty years have consciously reversed direction. The improvement in the fortunes of economic liberalism seems more than an 'accident of fashion'.

5. Reforming governments have appeared in every region of the world and from both the 'left' and the 'right' of the conventional political spectrum. They have included authoritarian regimes though there is a strong association between political and economic freedoms.

6. It is not true that coalitions of interests largely preclude economic liberalisation: otherwise, the reforms of recent years would not have taken place.

7. Liberal ideas have regained ground within the economics profession after a period from the 1930s to the 1970s when they were regarded as 'less central' than previously.

8. The 'balance of informed opinion' has also shifted to embrace liberal ideas. Politicians, civil servants and central bankers all came to support structural economic reforms from the mid-1980s onwards - even before the collapse of communism powerfully reinforced the liberal cause.

9. Despite the spread of liberal ideas, liberalism has a 'chronic weakness' because its conscious adherents are so few. In most countries majority opinion remains hostile to 'leaving it to the market', partly because of the continuing hold of pre-economic ideas.

10. Although events and continuing technical progress will probably continue to favour the liberal cause, anti-liberal ideas are still strong. Extending market reforms into areas so far untouched by liberalisation will be difficult. Hence the fortunes of economic liberalism in the early twenty first century are 'clouded and in doubt'.

The Institute of Economic Affairs

2 Lord North Street, Westminster, London SW1P 3LB
Telephone: 0171 799 3745 Facsimile: 0171 799 2137
E-mail: iea@iea.org.uk Internet: http://www.iea.org.uk   ISBN 0-255 36419-9

£12.00